I Know an Astronaut

My Uncle Bill is an astronaut.
He takes me to the Space Center.
There I see how he practices for his space
 trips.
No wonder he knows just what to do on the
 moon.

A COMMUNITY HELPER BOOK

I Know an Astronaut

by Michael Rubinger

Illustrated by Joel Snyder

G. P. Putnam's Sons   New York

Text copyright © 1972 by Michael Rubinger
Illustrations copyright © 1972 by Joel Snyder

All rights reserved. Published simultaneously in
Canada by Longmans Canada Limited, Toronto.
SBN: GB 399-60713-7
SBN: TR 399-20281-3

Library of Congress Catalog Card Number: 74–166989

PRINTED IN THE UNITED STATES OF AMERICA
06208

"Anybody home?"

I run to the door.
"Here's Uncle Bill!" I shout.

"Have fun," Mother tells me.

"See you in orbit," calls Dad.

6

Uncle Bill and I laugh.

Today he is taking me to the **Space Center**.

He is an **astronaut**.

Soon he will make a trip to the moon.

Uncle Bill looks very strong and brave in his uniform.
I know he is one of the best pilots in the Air Force.
He was chosen from many men all over the country to be an astronaut.

"Uncle Bill," I say, "I would like to learn to fly.
Then maybe I can be an astronaut, too."

"That's a start," he says.
"But there's more to being an astronaut than just knowing how to fly.
You'll also have to learn all about **rockets**.
And space travel.
And how to live in space."

"You mean I have to go to school?" I ask.

"I'm afraid so." My uncle laughs.
"But it's not so bad.
There's lots of fun and excitement, too."

As we get to the Space Center, I can see many buildings.
There is a big fence around them.
A man who looks like a policeman stops us at the gate.
My uncle shows him a card.
"OK, Major Wilson," the man says.
"You may go in."

"The Space Center is a very special place," Uncle Bill tells me.

"We have secret information.
And many expensive machines that are easily broken and hard to replace.
So only people with cards like mine can come inside."

My uncle takes me into a long, low building.
It has many rooms with glass walls.
There are a lot of busy people.

Uncle Bill says, "In these rooms we make
believe we are flying in space.
We practice everything over and over again.
What we learn here may save our lives when
we *really* go to the moon."

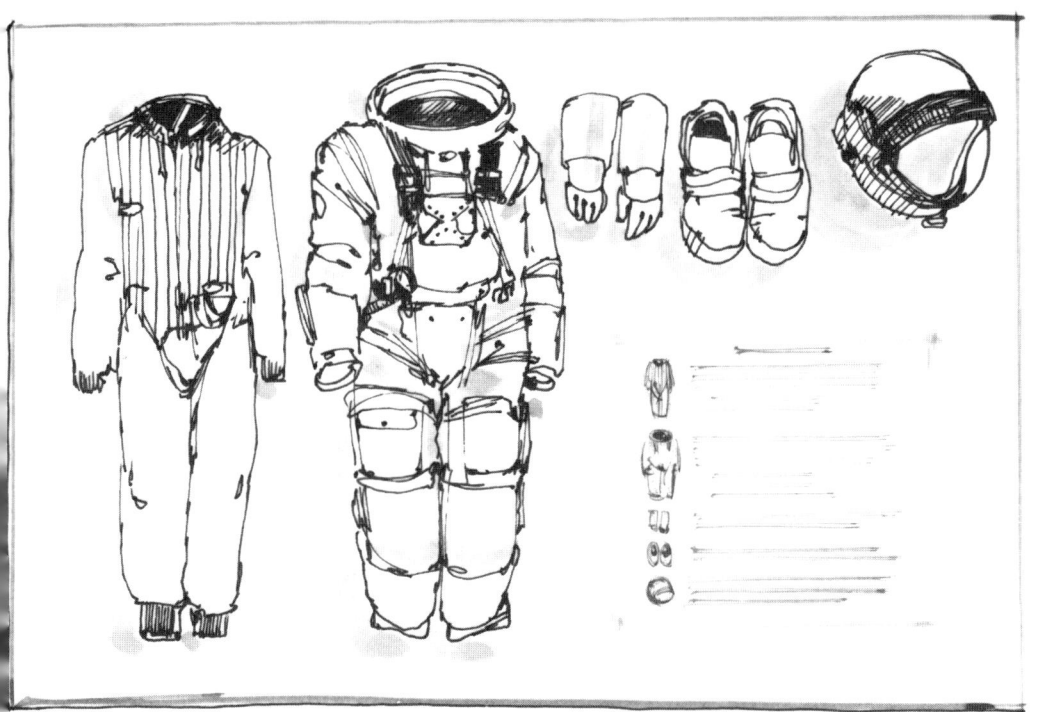

In the first room I see a **space suit** hanging on the wall.

"Is that what you will wear on the moon, Uncle Bill?"

"That's right, Tommy.
On the moon it is either so hot or so cold that a man from Earth could not live without a space suit.
It protects me from freezing to death or burning up.

"A space suit is big and heavy.
It weighs 180 pounds!
An astronaut spends many hours learning to walk and to climb in and out of the **spacecraft** with his suit on.

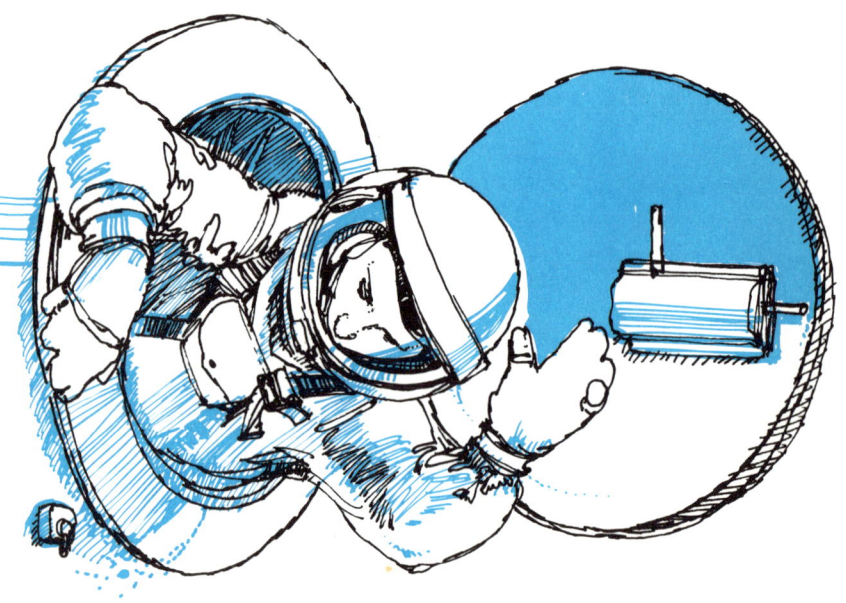

"Remember, too, that in space there is no air to breathe.
So an astronaut brings his own air with him.
He carries it in a big tank on his back, just as a skin diver does when he goes underwater."

We walk down the hall to another room.
Inside is a big machine.

It is spinning like a merry-go-round, but
 much, much faster.
My uncle tells me it is called a **centrifuge**.
"What is it for?" I ask.

"The centrifuge helps us practice our take-off. In a real **blast-off**, the rocket moves very quickly away from the Earth.
The pull of **gravity** makes the men inside feel very heavy.
They feel so heavy they can hardly move.
When we whirl around in the centrifuge, we feel the same way."

"I learned about gravity in school," I tell Uncle Bill. "It is the force that holds everything down on Earth.

People and cars and everything would just fly away if there were no pull of gravity.
We can't feel it, but it's always pulling on us.
It's what gives us weight.
I know that the Earth's pull of gravity on me is fifty-four pounds because that's how much I weigh."

"One thing you should also remember, Tommy, is that there is gravity on the moon just as there is on Earth.

But the moon's gravity is much less than the Earth's.

If you weigh fifty-four pounds on Earth, you will weigh only about nine pounds on the moon!

"As our rocket moves away from Earth, there
   is less and less gravity.
Soon we begin to feel very light.
After a while we have almost no weight at
   all, and we can float just like a balloon.
This is called **weightlessness**."

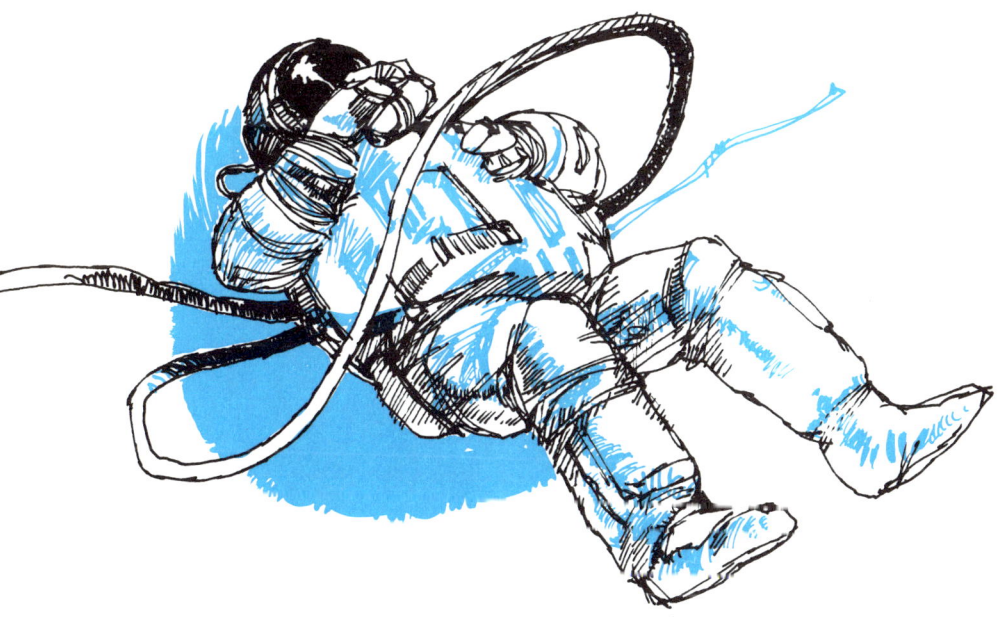

Weightlessness sounds like fun, I think to
   myself.
I can just see myself floating around through
   space.

But there is something I don't understand.
"Uncle Bill," I say.
"When I see astronauts on TV, they aren't floating around."

"No," he replies.
"They are wearing seat belts to hold them down so that they can fly the rocket.

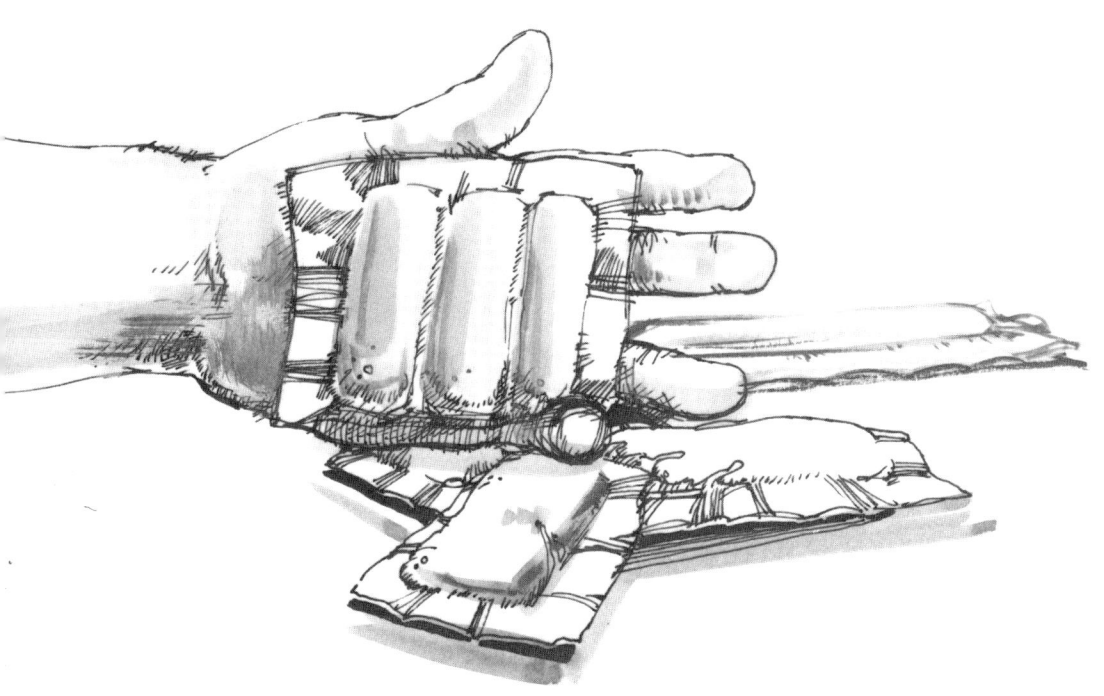

"Everything in space would float away if it were not tied down.
Even the food off our plates!
That is why we put all our food in special packages like these."

Uncle Bill shows me some little packages of food wrapped in plastic.

"You eat that?" I make a face.
"It looks awful."

"It is!" My uncle laughs.
"But we make it soft with water from a little hose.
We drink from the hose, too.
Water in a glass would just float right out.

"When we finish eating, we put these plastic wrappers in closed garbage containers.
If we did not, the spacecraft would soon be filled with floating garbage."

"I've heard about air pollution." I laugh.
"But I never heard of *space* pollution before."

"It may sound funny," Uncle Bill says.
"But it's really very serious.
"Say, Tommy," Uncle Bill asks,
"would you like to ride in a spacecraft?"

"Sure!" I reply. "But how could I do that?"

"Climb into this machine and I'll show you,"
  my uncle replies.
"We can't take a real ride, but almost.
This is a **spacecraft simulator**.
All these instruments and controls are exactly
  like the ones in the **Apollo**.
And they really work.

"When the simulator is turned on, it moves and makes turns and makes you feel as if you were flying in space.

In this simulator, we run through the entire trip, from take-off to landing.

We pretend it's the real thing.

We can eat, sleep, watch the controls, work the machines, and talk on the radio.

"When we practice for a moon flight, we stay in the simulator for nine days. That's about how long the real flight takes.

"We test every possible thing that could go wrong on a flight. Then we see if we can fix it. That way, if there is a problem during the real flight, we will know what to do.

"During a flight, if we want to slow down or speed up, we fire the rockets that are attached to the outside of the spacecraft. This is called a **burn**."

"How does a burn make you go faster?"
I ask.

My uncle thinks for a moment.
Then he asks, "If you have a balloon full of air and you let it go, what happens?"

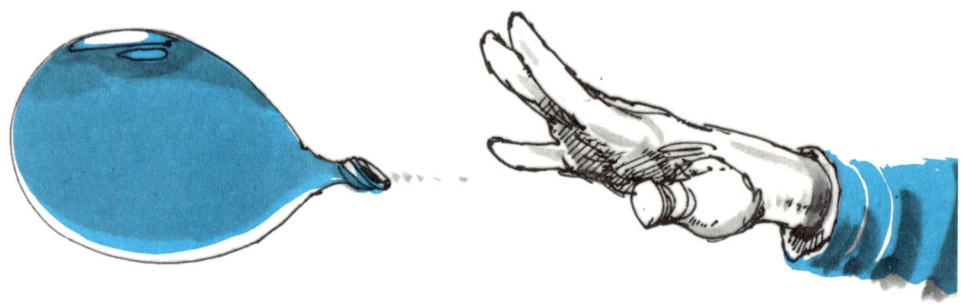

"The air comes out and the balloon shoots away," I reply.

"Right," says Uncle Bill.
"Firing the rockets on the spacecraft is like letting the air out of the balloon.
The rockets fire in one direction, pushing the spacecraft in the other direction."

Looking out the front window of the simulator, I can see the Earth and many tiny stars all around it.

Just for a moment, I think I'm really in space!

Of course, I'm only looking at a big movie screen.

"There are no maps or compasses in space travel," my uncle tells me.
"We can tell where we are by looking at the stars.
We can navigate our course by the stars, much like the early explorers who first sailed to America.

"On the screen, you can see how the Earth looks from space.
You can see whole continents and oceans.
From up here you can look at the clouds below and tell where it's raining and where the sun is shining on Earth.

"Every once in a while on a space trip, you can even see other man-made **satellites** that are orbiting the Earth. Did you know that right now there are more than four thousand of these satellites in space?"

"Could you crash into one of them on your moon flight, Uncle Bill?" I ask.

"No, I don't think so," replies my uncle. "There is still enough empty space for all our **flight patterns**.

"But in a few years that could become a problem."

"What does it feel like when you are really flying in space?" I ask my uncle.

"It's like flying in an airplane, Tommy, only better," he replies.
"Airplanes sometimes bounce in the wind.
There is no wind in space so the spacecraft doesn't bounce.
The jet plane I flew in the Air Force went 600 miles an hour.
This spacecraft flies thirty times faster than that.
But you can't really feel the difference when you're flying because the ride is so smooth.

"We work very hard during the flight. We are always working the instruments, keeping records of the trip in our **logbook**, and reporting back to Earth on the radio.

"When we're not too busy, we take pictures that you see on your TV back home.

"One problem on long flights is that we can't get up and move around.

If you've ever taken a long ride in a car, you know how uncomfortable it is to sit for a long time.

Of course, we can't stop and stretch our legs the way you can on a car trip.

"We use special machines to exercise our legs and arms.
That way our bodies don't get too stiff from the long hours of sitting.

"Well, Tommy, it looks as if we're about ready to land on the moon.
But we'll have to go to another building for that."

We leave the simulator.
As we head for the moon building, Uncle Bill tells me, "Landing on the moon is the hardest part of the whole trip.

"As our spacecraft nears the moon, we 'burn' the rockets.

The spacecraft slows down and goes into **orbit** around the moon.

Then a tiny spacecraft, called the **lunar module**, breaks away from the big **command ship** and flies down for the landing.

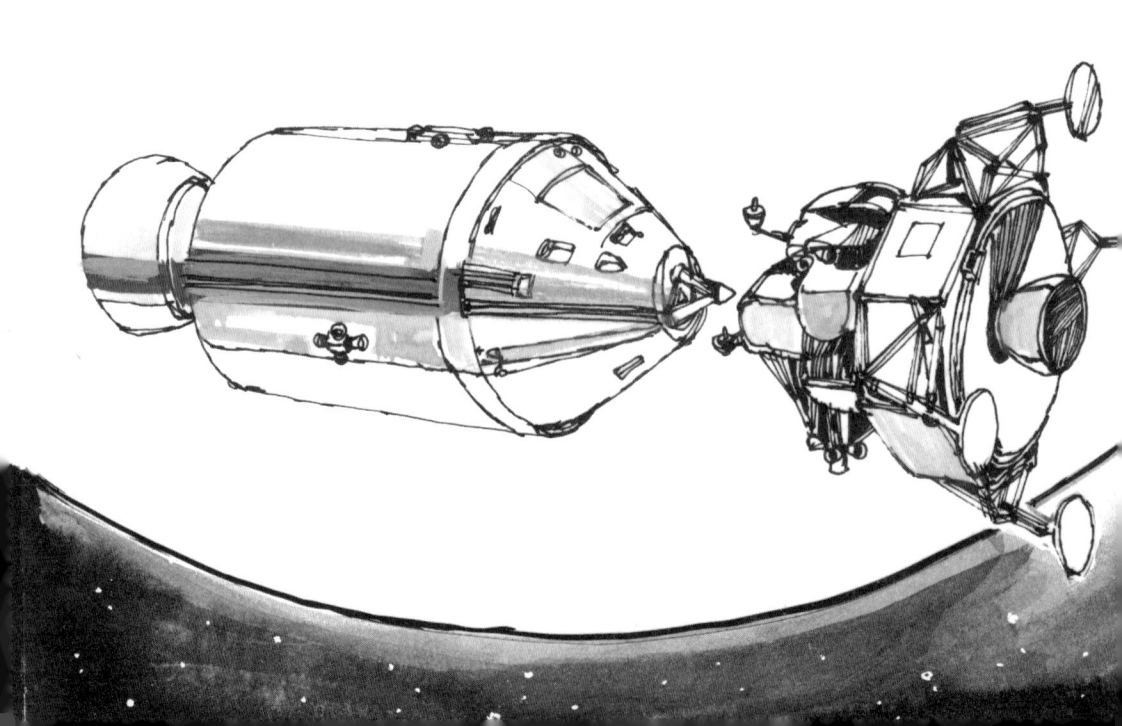

"Later, when we're ready to leave, the lunar module blasts off from the moon and **docks** with the command ship again for the trip home.
The lunar module doesn't have enough power to get back to Earth by itself.
If something goes wrong and we can't dock with the command ship, the lunar module could not get back to Earth."

The door to the moon building opens.
I can't believe it.
It's just as if we have landed on the moon!
There are the **craters** and the lunar module.

Just as they were when I saw Neil Armstrong make the first walk on the moon.
There's even an astronaut in a space suit collecting **moon rocks**.
Out behind the moon building, I see a huge tank filled with water.
Floating in the water is a **space capsule** like the ones I have seen on TV.

My uncle says, "This is where we practice returning to Earth.
We call this **reentry**.
When we return from space flights, we land in the ocean.

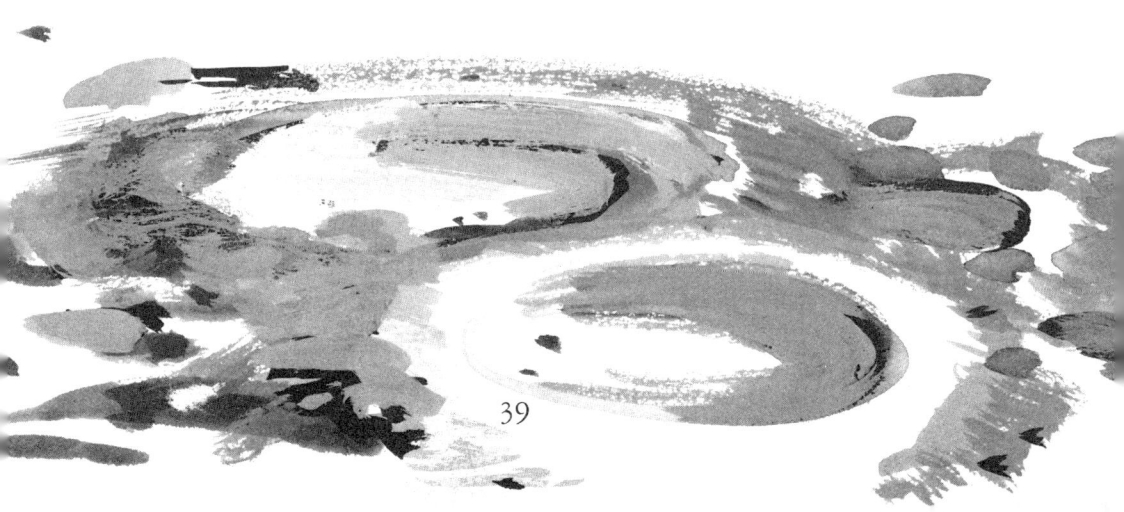

"These astronauts are practicing how to get out of the spacecraft after it lands. If the ocean waves are rough, the capsule could turn over. So we practice how to get out even if the capsule is upside down."

"Don't you get help from men in helicopters when you land?" I ask.

"Yes," answers my uncle. "They are Navy **frogmen** from the rescue ship.

After we practice in this tank, we go out in the ocean and work with the frogmen. We do everything just like a real mission.

"First the frogmen jump into the water from the helicopters.

Then they tie balloons to the capsule to keep it from turning over.

It's like putting a life jacket on the capsule.

But it's not called a life jacket; we call it a **flotation collar**.

Once this is done, the astronauts climb out and get into **a rubber raft**.

"Then a **basket** is dropped on a rope from the helicopter, and the astronauts are pulled up to safety."

"Uncle Bill, what would happen if you got lost or something and you didn't land in the ocean?"

"That's hard to say, Tommy, because so far it has never happened.
But during training we do learn how to survive in the jungle and the desert just in case a spacecraft does land there by mistake.

"Well, Tommy, that's the end of our moon flight and our tour of the Space Center," Uncle Bill says.
"Today you have been as close to making a moon flight as you could be without being a real astronaut.
Now you see that everything we do on a moon mission, even walking on the moon's surface, we have already practiced many times before here at the center."

A month from now I'll be sitting in front of the TV watching the huge Apollo rocket blasting off for the moon.
I know it's a long, hard, and dangerous trip.
But I won't worry about Uncle Bill.
I know he's been there before.

GLOSSARY

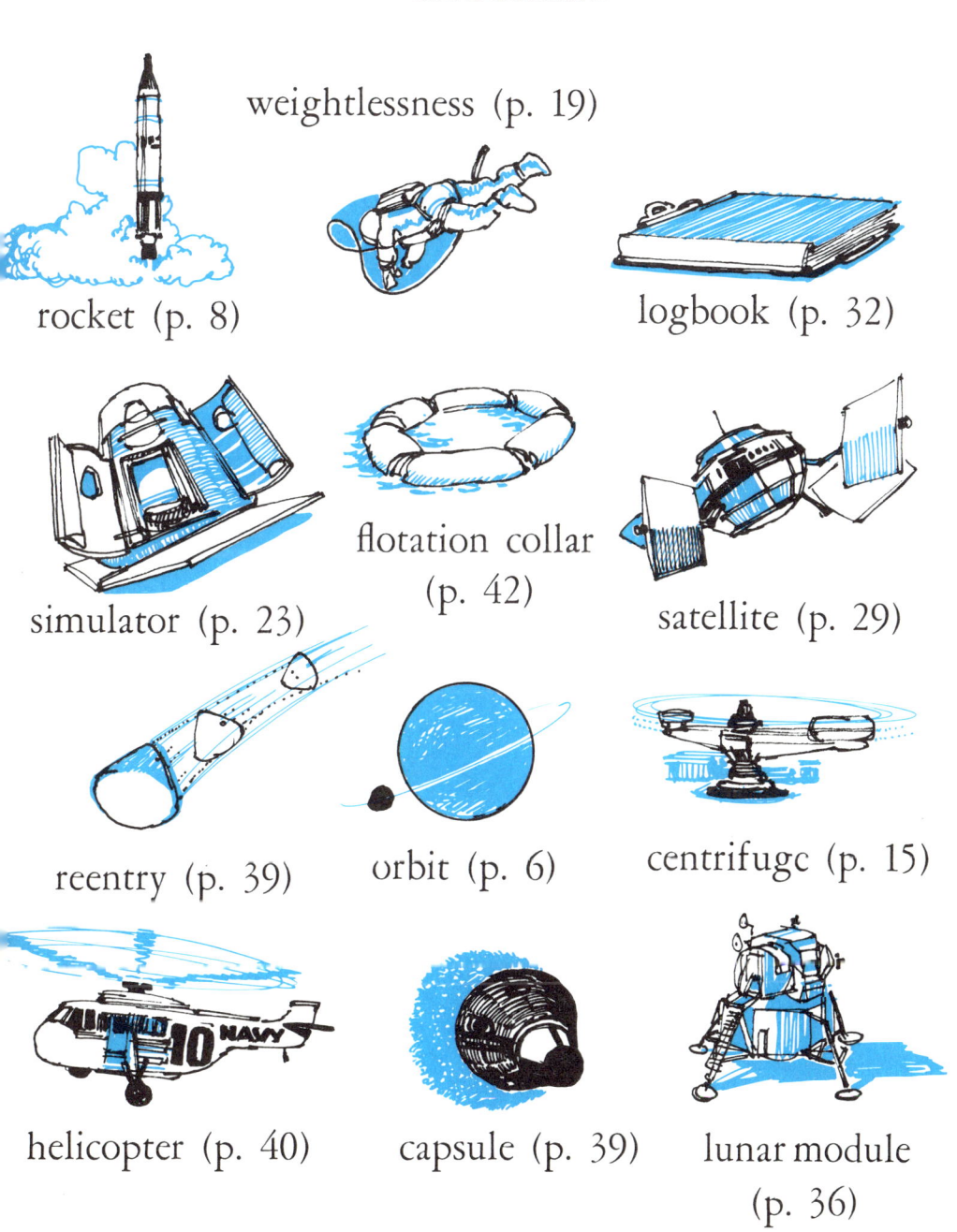

rocket (p. 8)

weightlessness (p. 19)

logbook (p. 32)

simulator (p. 23)

flotation collar (p. 42)

satellite (p. 29)

reentry (p. 39)

orbit (p. 6)

centrifuge (p. 15)

helicopter (p. 40)

capsule (p. 39)

lunar module (p. 36)

A Community Helper Book

I Know a Policeman
by Barbara Williams
Illustrated by Charles Dougherty

I Know a Librarian
by Virginia Voight
Illustrated by Haris Petie

I Know a Fireman
by Barbara Williams
Illustrated by Paula Brynes

I Know a Mayor
by Barbara Williams
Illustrated by Charles Dougherty

I Know a Postman
by Lorraine Henriod
Illustrated by Haris Petie

I Know a Teacher
by Naomi Buchheimer
Illustrated by Leonard Shortall

I Know a House Builder
by Polly Bolian and Marilyn Schima
Illustrated by Polly Bolian

I Know a Truck Driver
written and illustrated
by J. A. Evans

I Know an Animal Doctor
by Chika A. Iritani
Illustrated by Gerald McCann

I Know an Astronaut
by Michael Rubinger
Illustrated by Joel Snyder

I Know a Garageman
by Barbara Williams
Illustrated by Marvin Besunder

I Know a Bank Teller
by Barbara Williams
Illustrated by Albert Micale

I Know a Zoo Keeper
by Lorraine Henriod
Illustrated by Jane Evans

I Know a Nurse
by Polly Bolian and Marilyn Schima
Illustrated by Polly Bolian

I Know an Airline Pilot
by Muriel Stanek
Illustrated by Paul Frame

I Know a Baker
by Chika A. Iritani
Illustrated by Jane Evans

I Know a Grocer
by Lorraine Henriod
Illustrated by Albert Orbaan

I Know a Dairyman
by Muriel Stanek
Illustrated by Charles Dougherty

I Know a Weatherman
by Barbara Williams
Illustrated by Russell Hoover

I Know a Bus Driver
by Genevieve S. Gray
Illustrated by Charles Dougherty